Pigs/Cerdos

DISCARD

By JoAnn Early Mack

Reading Consultant: Jeanne Clic
Director, Roberts Wesleyan College L

CHICAGO PUBLIC LIBRA
THOMAS HUGHES
400 SOUTH STATE STREET
CHICAGO, ILLINOIS 60605

Please visit our web site at **www.garethstevens.com**.
For a free catalog describing our list of high-quality books,
call 1-877-542-2595 (USA) or 1-800-387-3178 (Canada).
Our fax: 1-877-542-2596

Library of Congress Cataloging-in-Publication Data

Macken, JoAnn Early, 1953–
    (Pigs. Spanish & English)
    Pigs = Cerdos / by JoAnn Early Macken.
       p. cm.— (Animals that live on the farm = Animales de la granja)
    Includes bibliographical references and index.
    ISBN-10: 1-4339-2431-5   ISBN-13: 978-1-4339-2431-6 (lib. bdg.)
    ISBN-10: 1-4339-2475-7   ISBN-13: 978-1-4339-2475-0 (soft cover)
    1. Swine—Juvenile literature. I. Title. II. Title: Cerdos.
SF395.5.M3312 2010
636.4—dc22   2009011972

This edition first published in 2010 by
Weekly Reader® Books
An Imprint of Gareth Stevens Publishing
1 Reader's Digest Road
Pleasantville, NY 10570-7000 USA

Copyright © 2010 by Gareth Stevens, Inc.

Executive Managing Editor: Lisa M. Herrington
Senior Editor: Barbara Bakowski
Project Management: Spooky Cheetah Press
Cover Designers: Jennifer Ryder-Talbot and Studio Montage
Production: Studio Montage
Translators: Tatiana Acosta and Guillermo Gutiérrez
Library Consultant: Carl Harvey, Library Media Specialist, Noblesville, Indiana

Photo credits: Cover, pp. 1, 5, 7, 17 Shutterstock; pp. 9, 21 © Alan and Sandy Carey;
pp. 11, 15, 19 © Norvia Behling; p. 13 © James P. Rowan

All rights reserved. No part of this book may be reproduced, stored in a retrieval system,
or transmitted in any form or by any means, electronic, mechanical, photocopying, recording,
or otherwise, without the prior written permission of the copyright holder. For permission, contact
permissions@gspub.com.

Printed in the United States of America

1 2 3 4 5 6 7 8 9 14 13 12 11 10 09

R0422845307

Table of Contents

- - - - - - - - - - - - - - - -

Contenido

CHICAGO PUBLIC LIBRARY
THOMAS HUGHES
400 SOUTH STATE STREET
CHICAGO, ILLINOIS 60605

Boldface words appear in the glossary./
Las palabras en **negrita** aparecen en el glosario.

Little and Big Pigs

A baby pig is a **piglet**. Piglets snuggle close to stay warm.

- - - - - - - - - - - - - - - -

Cerdos pequeños y grandes

Una cría de cerdo es un **lechón**. Los lechones se acurrucan todos juntos para darse calor.

piglets/
lechones

Piglets drink milk from their mother. A grown female pig is called a **sow**. The piglets squeal as they crowd against their mother.

Los lechones beben la leche de su madre. La hembra adulta recibe el nombre de **cerda**. Los lechones se agolpan contra la madre lanzando chillidos.

sow/
cerda

Ready to Eat

Grown pigs eat almost anything! When they are outside, pigs eat roots, nuts, and plants.

- - - - - - - - - - - - - -

Ganas de comer

¡Los cerdos adultos comen casi cualquier cosa! Cuando están al aire libre, los cerdos comen raíces, frutos secos y plantas.

8

On a farm, pigs are fed grain. They also eat grass and vegetables. They may even eat leftovers from the farmer's dinner!

- - - - - - - - - - - - - - -

En una granja, los cerdos son alimentados con grano. También comen hierba y verduras. ¡Llegan a comerse hasta los restos de la cena de los granjeros!

grain/
grano

A Very Clever Animal

Pigs stay cool by lying in water. Pigs also **wallow** in mud. They roll in mud to cool off and to keep from getting a sunburn.

- - - - - - - - - - - - - -

Un animal muy listo

Los cerdos se refrescan echándose en el agua. También evitan el calor y se protegen del sol **revolcándose** en el lodo.

Pigs can hear well, but they do not see well. Their eyes are small.

- - - - - - - - - - - - - -

Los cerdos tienen buen oído, pero no ven bien. Sus ojos son pequeños.

Pigs have a good sense of smell. A pig's nose is called a **snout**.

- - - - - - - - - - - - - -

Los cerdos tienen un buen sentido del olfato. La nariz de un cerdo se llama **hocico**.

snout/
hocico

Pigs are smart animals. They can learn to do tricks. This pig drinks water from a hose!

- - - - - - - - - - - - - - -

Los cerdos son unos animales muy inteligentes. Es posible enseñarles a hacer trucos. ¡Este cerdo está bebiendo de una manguera!

Pigs grow faster than any other farm animal. They can grow very big.

- - - - - - - - - - - - - -

Los cerdos crecen más rápido que cualquier otro animal de granja. Pueden ponerse muy grandes.

Fast Facts/Datos básicos

Height/ Altura	about 3 feet (1 meter) at the shoulder/ unos 3 pies (1 metro) en la cruz
Length/ Longitud	about 5 feet (2 meters) nose to tail/ unos 5 pies (2 metros) de nariz a cola
Weight/ Peso	about 250 pounds (113 kilograms)/ unas 250 libras (113 kilogramos)
Diet/ Dieta	roots, nuts, plants, grain, grass, and vegetables/ raíces, frutos secos, plantas, grano, hierba y vegetales
Average life span/ Promedio de vida	up to 15 years/ hasta 15 años

Glossary/Glosario

piglet: a baby pig

snout: the front part of an animal's head, including the nose

sow: a grown female pig

wallow: roll around

- - - - - - - - - - - - - - - - - - - -

cerda: hembra adulta del cerdo

hocico: parte delantera de la cabeza de un animal, incluyendo la nariz

lechón: cría de cerdo

revolcarse: echarse y dar vueltas

For More Information/Más información

Books/Libros

Animals at the Farm/Animales de la granja.
English-Spanish Foundations (series). Gladys Rosa-Mendoza
(me+mi publishing, 2004)

Pigs. Down on the Farm (series). Hannah Ray
(Crabtree Publishing, 2008)

Web Sites/Páginas web

Pigs, Pork, Swine Facts/Datos sobre cerdos y puercos
oklahoma4h.okstate.edu/aitc/lessons/extras/facts/swine.html
Read fascinating facts about pigs./Lean fascinantes datos
sobre los cerdos.

Welcome to Our Farm/Bienvenidos a nuestra granja
www.pork4kids.com/kids/farm_tour.asp
Take a virtual tour of a real pig farm./Hagan una visita virtual
a una auténtica granja de cerdos.

Publisher's note to educators and parents: Our editors have carefully reviewed these web sites to ensure that they are suitable for children. Many web sites change frequently, however, and we cannot guarantee that a site's future contents will continue to meet our high standards of quality and educational value. Be advised that children should be closely supervised whenever they access the Internet.

Nota de la editorial a los padres y educadores: Nuestros editores han revisado con cuidado las páginas web para asegurarse de que son apropiadas para niños. Sin embargo, muchas páginas web cambian con frecuencia, y no podemos garantizar que sus contenidos futuros sigan conservando nuestros elevados estándares de calidad y de interés educativo. Tengan en cuenta que los niños deben ser supervisados atentamente siempre que accedan a Internet.

Index/Índice

About the Author

JoAnn Early Macken is the author of two rhyming picture books, *Sing-Along Song* and *Cats on Judy*, and more than 80 nonfiction books for children. Her poems have appeared in several children's magazines. She lives in Wisconsin with her husband and their two sons.

- - - - - - - - - - - - - - - - - - - -

Información sobre la autora

JoAnn Early Macken ha escrito dos libros de rimas con ilustraciones, *Sing-Along Song* y *Cats on Judy*, y más de ochenta libros de no ficción para niños. Sus poemas han sido publicados en varias revistas infantiles. Vive en Wisconsin con su esposo y sus dos hijos.